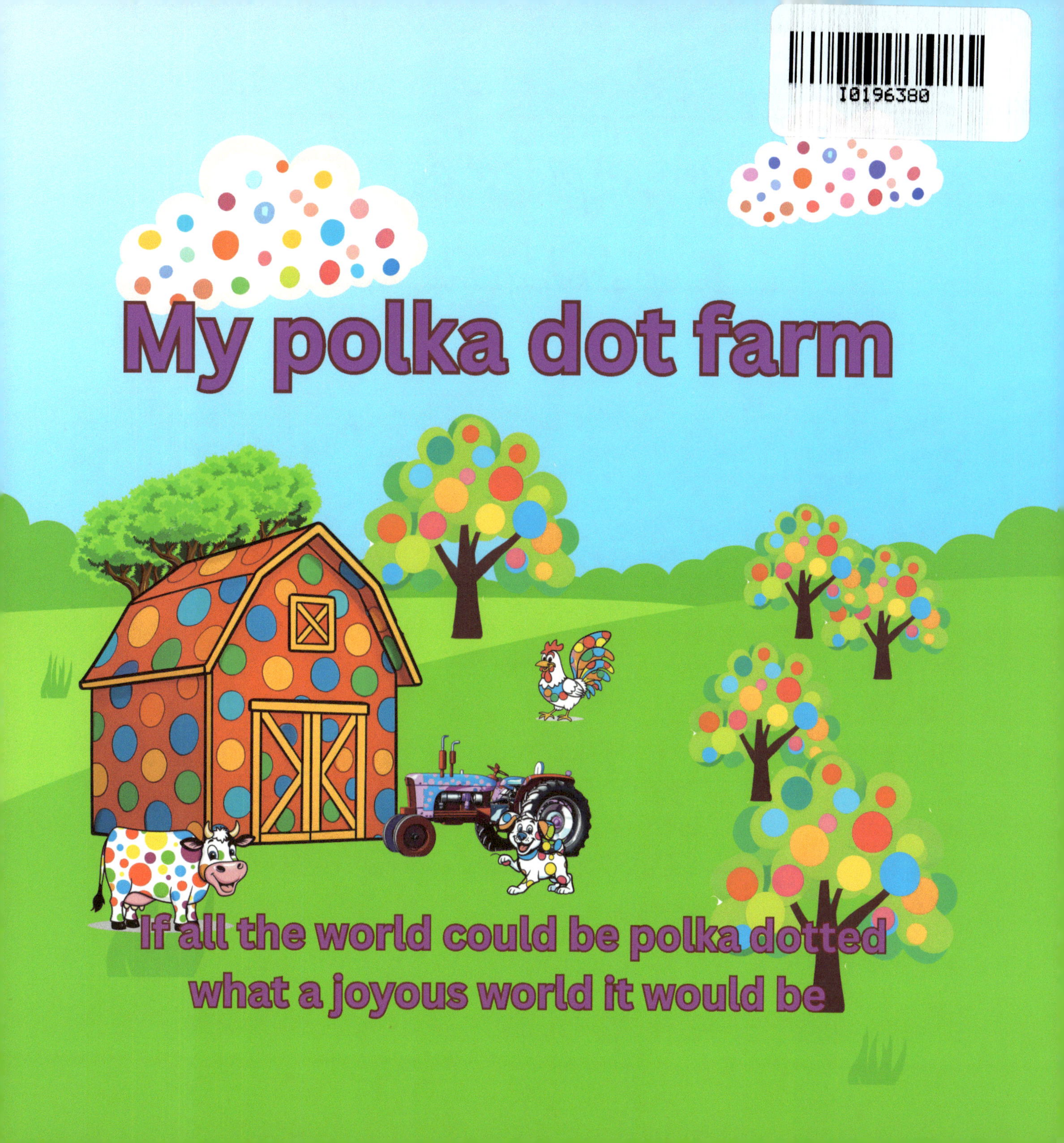

My polka dot farm

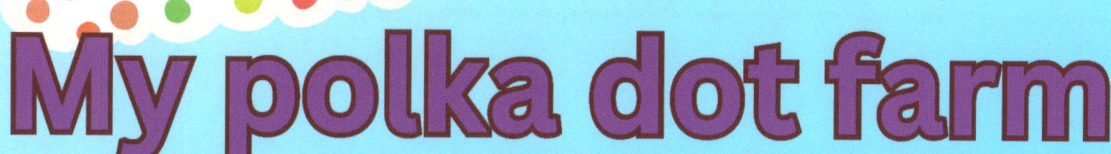

If all the world could be polka dotted
what a joyous world it would be

I want a polka dot farm when I grow up

And my best friend will be a polka dot pup

A polka dot rooster and some polka dot chickens

A polka dot barn with polka dot cows

Some polka dot pigs
and some polka dot sows

I'll have polka dot trees with apples on top

And lots of polka dot bunnies that love to hop

2 polka dot mice named Wiggles and Scrat

A pair of polka dot squirrels and a polka dot cat

I'll have 4 polka dot llamas and of course

Every polka dot farm needs a polka dot horse

I'll have a big blue pond with polka dot ducks

And my farm needs
2 polka dot trucks

And polka dot sheep with polka dot toes

I'll have a polka dot donkey that eats polka dot hay

And polka dot goats that run and play

I'll grow polka dot carrots and polka dot peas

Collect jars of honey from polka dot bees

And a polka dot wagon
with a wheel that wobbles

Some day I'll have my farm just like I said

Until then I'll dream in my polka dot bed

More titles by Anita Smith

Marty the Moose is Making Maple Muffins
Sal the Cape Breton Seagull
Luna Loon's Legendary Eleven Layer Leafy Lasagna
The Easter Farmer
Why do Reindeer Wear Socks
The Crafty elephant
The Grooviest Goat

The Color Series
The things that I think when I think about pink
The things that I think when I think about blue
The things that I think when I think about yellow

Maisy wants a Moo for Christmas
Once in a Blue Moose

www.ingramcontent.com/pod-product-compliance
Lightning Source LLC
Chambersburg PA
CBHW042128040426
42450CB00002B/116